The Perfect Gift

Rohan Henry

Stewart, Tabori & Chang | New York

I'm Leo Rabbit

and this is Lisa Rabbit.

Lisa and I have known each other for a long time. But I wanted to let her know somehow that she was my best friend.

The next day I went to visit her.

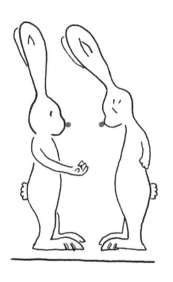

"I have a surprise for you," I said.

"It's the first leaf of autumn."

"This leaf is truuuly beautiful," said Lisa.
"My, how clever you are."
But a strong wind came and blew my present
away. The first leaf of autumn was forever
lost.

All the leaves fell from the trees...

and the days grew colder.

Then I found another gift special enough for Lisa.

"I have a surprise for you," I said.

"It's the most delicate snowflake of winter."

"This snowflake is truuuly beautiful," said Lisa.
"My, how thoughtful you are."
But the warmth of my hand melted away the most delicate gift.

Soon the flowers started to bloom.
This will be the best gift yet, I
thought!

"I have a surprise for you," I told Lisa.

" <u>I</u>t's the most radiant butterfly of spring."

"This butterfly is truuuly beautiful," said Lisa.
"My, how kind you are."
But the glow of the sun attracted the butterfly and it flew away. The most radiant butterfly of spring was forever lost.

"Wait, Leo, I have something important to tell you," said Lisa. But I was too busy to listen.

Instead, I set off in search of the perfect gift.

I searched the highest mountain.

And I searched the lowest valley.

I searched far.

And I searched near.

But I couldn't find the perfect gift, a gift that would last.

Finally, I returned home with no gift
at all.

Soon after, Lisa came to visit me.

"Let me see your hand," she said.

"No, "I said. "I searched through the seasons. I searched high, low, far, and near. And I still haven't found the perfect gift for you."

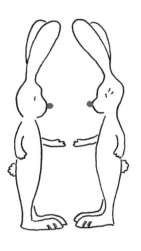

"Leo, I don't want the perfect gift.
All I want is to hold the hand
of my best friend."